W9-CSG-839

The Theatre Arts
Audition
Book for Men

E.P.L. — MNA

The Theatre Arts
Audition
Book for Men

Compiled by Annika Bluhm

A Theatre Arts Book

Routledge • New York

Published in the USA and Canada in 2003 by
Routledge
29 West 35th Street
New York, NY 10001
www.routldge-ny.com

Routledge is an imprint of the Taylor & Francis Group

Copyright in this selection © 2002 by Annika Bluhm

First printed in Great Britain in 1989 by Methuen Drama
This revised and updated edition first published in 2003 by
Methuen Publishing Limited
215 Vauxhall Bridge Road
London SW1V 1EJ

Printed in the United States of America on acid-free paper.

These extracts are fully protected by copyright. Any enquiries concerning the rights for pro-fessional or amateur stage production, broadcasting, readings, etc. should be made to the authors' agents and not to the publisher.

This book is sold subject to the condition that it shall not, by way of trade or otherwise, be lent, resold, hired out, or otherwise circulated in any form of binding or cover other than that in which it is published and without a similar condition, including this condition, being imposed on the subsequent purchaser.

10 9 8 7 6 5 4 3 2 1

Library of Congress Cataloging-in-Publication Data
The theatre arts audition book for men / complied by Annika Bluhm.
   p. cm.
   "Theatre Arts book."
   ISBN 0-87830-172-0 (alk. Paper)
1. Acting. 2. Monologues. 3. Acting—Audtions. 4. Drama—20th century. 5. Men—Drama. I. Bluhm, Annika.

PN 2080.T47 2003
822'.0450891—dc21   2002036978

Contents

Thank you to Andrew, Griffin and Arden Farrow.

Introduction

In the course of compiling this book I spoke to a number of directors working in various areas of theatre, from drama schools to the National Theatre. Nearly everyone agreed that an actor's most important attribute was self-knowledge. Self-knowledge can be expressed in a variety of ways: through wit, intelligence, verbal and physical dexterity, an assertive, as opposed to an aggressive manner.

There is a great difference in approach to auditioning in Britain and the United States. In America cut-throat competition has engendered a highly professional attitude. Actors tend to arrive fully prepared for an audition, on time, with well-rehearsed speeches from plays that they have taken the time to read in their entirety. In contrast directors spoke about the appalling diffidence of many actors in Britain, who arrived in no way prepared, appearing to feel that the audition was something of an imposition and that performing was the last thing in the world they wanted to do.

Directors were keen to emphasize the fact that an audition is not a test but a meeting between the actor and director to assess the possibility of working together. Many felt that auditioning should be more of a two-way process and that actors should accept more power or responsibility for themselves when auditioning. In other words, actors should not be tempted to play down their own intelligence, to act according to what they think the director wants, but to see themselves as professionals.

Opinions differ as to how much an actor can show about the way he/she works in an audition. One felt that it was a genuine opportunity for an actor to display their work; another, that little could actually be revealed by the presentation of a speech – auditioning being an artificial performing situation – and that the actor should concentrate on presenting *themselves* as well as possible, on maximizing their presence. Clearly in an ideal audition one should do both. One should be clear, concise and, equally important, unpretentious. One director talked of avoiding the temptation to be arch. Another was looking for 'assurance with natural reticence', which she went on to explain as including the director in the audition in an open way, talking with, rather than at, him or her.

Most key points as regards the selection and presentation of the audition piece are common sense, but easy to overlook in the attempt to impress. For instance it would be unwise to attempt a speech using a particular accent unless it was well within your capabilities and it would be sensible to choose a role within your own age-range. In the event of an audition being for a specific role, select a pertinent piece: if the production is to be a comedy, present a comic speech. It should be emphasized that there is no substitute, when preparing an audition speech, for reading the play in its entirety.

Everybody acknowledged the advantages of doing a witty or comic piece mainly because they enjoyed being able to laugh. They felt that it was extremely hard for an actor to play a highly emotional scene in an audition without resorting to a good deal of tension, both physically and vocally.

How can you make auditioning a less nerve-racking affair? Most directors agreed on this. Get a good night's sleep, wear comfortable clothes, arrive early and find a quiet place to calm down and 'centre' yourself. Above all, everyone stressed, *have fun*!

Some speeches are amalgamated. This is indicated by punctuation: [. . .].

Road *by Jim Cartwright*

Road is an episodic play set in a street in Lancashire where unemployment and despair is rife. Throughout the play different characters reveal the state of their lives.

Skin is one of these characters. This speech is the only time Skin appears in the play. However, it is imperative to read the whole play to understand this character.

———————————

Lights come up on a **Young Man** *sitting on a wooden chair. A bare light bulb is dangling.*

Skin Om. He opens his eyes. He sees you. He wants to tell you the story. He feels the need to drift back on the tide of his memory, back, back, back. And I'm the lonely skinhead again. Jogging away, every day, to the best, to be the best. And the press-ups. And the sit-ups. And the 1-2-3, 1-2-3, 1-2-3, 1-2-3. And you've gotta be fit to fight, and I do, every Saturday night, with my friends at weekends, fight. Do you know about fighting? No. I'll tell you in my story. And I want to be the best skinhead and I want to give everything, every single thing, to the experience of the tingle. I'll tell you about the tingle later. And you've got to be fit to fight, and practise tactics every night.

(*He practises on an imaginary opponenet.*) Do you? I do?

(*Practises.*) Do you work in the asbestos factory? I did.

(*Practises. Stops.*) I'll explain.

He indicates the imaginary opponent.

My opponent! Anyone you like! City fan, the cunt that shagged Ricky's bird, Ted the Foreman, you choose. Targets!

Goes down on imaginary body.

Face, neck, beerbag, dick, shin, top of the foot. Today I want the neck, this vein here. I don't want to fuck Christine Dawson, I don't want my mother's love. I don't want to work at the engineering firm, I want the neck, this vein here.

(*Practises*.) Tactics, new techniques. What does he think? What do you think?

(*Strikes*.) You thought, he thought, the neck and that's that. The neck and that is that. Now I've told you about the three things you need to get to the experience of the tingle. One, fitness, told you. Two, tactics, told you. Three, new techniques, I told you. Now I'll tell you about the tingle.

He comes off the stage into the audience. This next bit should be improvised.

Well it's . . . you can't say it, can you . . .? It'll come when you're fighting. Sometimes in the middle, sometime beginning, sometime end, but it won't stay . . . it's like you are there, you are fighting, but 'you' are not there . . .

Pause.

You don't understand.

Pause.

Anyway, once you've had it you need it, and I thought that's all there was until that night, right, should I tell you about that night? No. I'll show you.

He leaps back on stage.

I came out the disco, last man to leave, all my lads had gone. I'd been talking to Mickey Isherwood the bouncer.

'See you Jim.'

'Aye, see you Ishey.'

Then I saw them. Skins. Bolton boot-boys. Skinheads. Some sitting on the wall, some standing. I moved off to the right.

'Eh, cunty.'

'Eh, git head.'

'Come 'ere.'

I looked at the moon. I heard the crack of denim, the scuffle down the wall, the pad and fall of the Dr Martens, pad, pad, pad. I closed my eyes. Pad, pad. As they moved in, pad, pad. I moved out. Pad, pad. I felt their breath . . . lifted one man by the chin . . . can you imagine it? Magnificent . . . they were scattering. Caught one man between thigh and calf, took him round to the ground, fingers up the nose, dragged a pace, nutted, lifted my fingers to pierce out his eyes when, to my surprise, I saw a figure watching, like a ghost, all pale in the light. He was laughing at me. Mocking my whole fucking life. I sprang; when I arrived, he'd gone. Too quick for me? No, I saw him disappear down a blind alley. I had him now. I had him now!

He was facing the wall in a sort of peeing position. I moved in to strike, my fist was like a golden orb in the wet night, I said it was night, I struck deep and dangerous and beautiful with a twist of the fist on the out. But he was only smiling, and he opened his eyes to me like two diamonds in the night. I said it was night, and said, 'Over to you, Buddha.'

Pause.

So now I just read the dharma. And when men at work pass the pornography, I pass it on and continue with the dharma. And when the man on the bus pushes I continue with the dharma.

Om.

Our Country's Good *by Timberlake Wertenbaker*

Our Country's Good takes as its basis the performance of Farquhar's *The Recruiting Officer* by a cast of convicts in Australia in 1789.

Ketch Freeman is a convict who has accepted the post of hangman and as such is hated and feared by the rest of the community. He hopes to be cast in the play and thereby gain popularity. He has come to beg the officer casting the play for a part.

Ketch James, Sir, James, Daniel, Patrick, after my three uncles. Good men they were too, didn't go to London. If my mother hadn't brought us to London, may God give peace to her soul and breathe pity into the hearts of hard women – because the docks are in London and if I hadn't worked on the docks, on that day, May 23rd, do you remember it, Sir? Shadwell Dock. If only we hadn't left, then I wouldn't have been there, then nothing would have happened, I wouldn't have become a coal heaver on Shadwell Dock and been there on the 23rd May when we refused to unload because they were paying us so badly Sir. I wasn't even near the sailor who got killed. He shouldn't have done the unloading, that was wrong of the sailors, but I didn't kill him, maybe one blow, not to look stupid, you know, just to show I was with the lads, even if I wasn't, but I didn't kill him. And they caught five at random Sir, and I was among the five, and they found the cudgel, but I just had that to look good, that's all, and when they said to me later you can hang or you can give the names what was I to do, what would you have done, Sir?

Ralph I wouldn't have been in that situation, Freeman.

Ketch To be sure, forgive me, Sir. I only told me the ones I saw. I didn't tell anything that wasn't true, death is a horrible thing, that poor sailor.

I understand, Sir, I understand. And when it happened again, here! And I had hopes of making a good life here. It's because I'm so friendly, see, so I go along, and then I'm the one who gets caught, that theft, I didn't do it, I was just there, keeping a look out, just to help some friends, you know. But when they say to you, hang or be hanged, what do you do? Someone has to do it. I try to do it well. God have mercy on the whore, the thief, the lame, surely he'll forgive me? – it's the women – they're without mercy – not like you and me, Sir, men. What I wanted to say, Sir, is that I heard them talking about the play.

Pause.

Some players came into our village once, they were loved like the angels, Lieutenant, like the angels. And the way the women watched them – the light of a spring dawn in their eyes.

Lieutenant.

I want to be an actor.

Treehouses *by Elizabeth Kuti*

During the war a young, presumably Jewish, boy avoiding deportation, is kept hidden by Magda, the local farmer's daughter. His presence is a source of strain between Magda and her lover, Stephen, who believes the boy should be given up to the authorities. Traumatised by what he has seen the boy is initially silent.

At this point in the play he explains to Magda, for the first time, his story.

_____

Boy I kept telling them we had to leave, I kept telling them – I've known for ages we had to go – all of us, we just should have gone, I kept telling them, but they wouldn't, they said we couldn't – but we knew, everyone knew. Every night central station was packed with people – we all knew about it – and trains going every night at three, four in the morning, trains going when there shouldn't have been any trains. I saw them ages ago, I walked past once at three in the morning, I was coming home from work in the restaurant, and I saw all these hundreds of people being jammed onto trains. And I looked up and all around the station in apartment blocks there were people looking out of windows, watching – and they all saw this going on – they saw, they knew – And everyone was talking about resettlement then, about persons being resettled in other provinces – but it didn't look right to me, I knew at the time it wasn't right – their faces were – the faces of the people – I don't know – it looked wrong to me. So I stopped and asked this guard – it was dark, he couldn't see my face so I asked him what was going on – where the trains were going – was this a resettlement programme, and what province were these people going to? And he laughed and said don't worry son, these trains are going east and all these people have got a one-way ticket, and I said what do you mean going east, to what province. And he laughed again and said, to another sort of province altogether [. . .] And I told my father this and I said I thought we should go then, we should have gone then, we should have walked out with nothing in our hands, we just should just have gone, we should have, we should have, we should have just walked –

Massage *by Michael Wilcox*

Rikki is a nineteen-year-old masseur. He arrives at the house of Doug ostensibly to give him 'just a massage'. Doug is suspected of having made sexual advances towards his girlfriend's son. As they talk Rikki begins to explain about his childhood and his adoption.

―――――――――――――――

Rikki   When I was ten. The people there, they got me all dressed up 'cause I was going to meet someone who wanted to adopt me. That's what the kids there dreamed of. Someone coming. Someone good . . . you know . . . to take you with them . . . to be your dad . . . take you on holidays and that . . . have your own room and your own things . . . possessions. Anyway, I was in this room and the door opened and this man and woman walked in, and I remember thinking, 'Bloody Hell! I'm not going off with them! The other kids'll think I'm daft!' But I did. Just for the afternoon. You don't clear off for good, just like that. They have to get to know you, to see if they like you. (. . .)

Caught the train to Southend. (. . .)

I'd been there before with the other kids . . . you know . . . from the Home. Seen the Wax Works. 'Torture through the Ages.' Not much cop. Supposed to be educational. Looked at the *Golden Hind*. Went on the racing cars by the pier. Great to be with someone with money to spend. When we was having a day out with the Home, we had to spend a lot of time just watching other kids having fun. Then we went to the Kursaal . . . big dippers and that. But we was running out of money. There was this incredible ride called The Toboggan. So mum and dad and me gets on this sledge thing and start to get hoisted up to the top of the Cresta Run. And once you're on it, there's no escape, even if you have a heart attack on the way up. 'Cause you can't see, when you pays your money, just how steep it is 'cause it goes right out of sight. But on the way up me mum starts screaming and dad's had a few drinks and says he feels sick and I was laughing. And when we gets to the top there's this lad with tattoos like a gipsy and he doesn't take the blindest notice of me dad, who threatens to bottle him. And the next thing we know, we're charging down this vertical run on a wooden tray at a hundred miles an hour. And we all screamed our heads off. And when we got to the top of the next hump, dad threw up and mum lost her hat! And I thought, 'If they can do this for me, maybe they're not so daft.'

Victoria *by David Greig*

Victoria comprises three different but interlinking plays that follow the political and social history of the last century through the experience of one rural community in Scotland. In this, the second play, Jimmy is the new laird, eager to sell his ancestral home and discover himself amongst the religious leaders of India. His mother disapproves of both his plans for the house and land and for himself.

In this speech Jimmy is explaining his reasons for wanting to travel to India and follow the teachings of the Vedic scriptures, collected by his father the former Laird.

Jimmy I'm writing a book about my father's work. Some of the thinking I've found – it's powerful. He was pushing the limits, exploring – thinking about nature – about life – you know – he was a rebel – I've inherited that. [. . .] Everyone's looking now – for some way to connect with something greater than ourselves – with nature. He was ahead of his time – this is what I'm finding out. [. . .] There is connection, and there's no connection. This is what the Vedas teach. [. . .] There are four ages, in history.
Each age is a decline on the previous.
In the first age everything that needs to be done, is done.
All men are good.
In the second age, men discover motivation, reward and punishment.
And have become corrupted.
In the third age,
Disunity prevails, difference emerges, and catastrophe begins.
In the last age, the age in which we're living,
Evil has become triumphant.
Civilisation recedes.
Marriage takes place between castes, women go with worthless men, blood ties disintegrate, commerce governs all meaning,
In due course time itself falls towards destruction.
Then there is rebirth, and the cycle begins again.
Each cycle, which last four million years, is one minute of one day in the life of Brahman. Brahman lives for a hundred years. When Brahman dies, the universe is reborn.
Everything is contained within the cycle of time.
The connection is in time.

Maydays *by David Edgar*

Maydays is a vast play spanning over twenty-five years and showing the fate of the socialist ideal through the eyes of three men, one of them Jeremy.

Over the course of the play Jeremy abandons his youthful communist principles to become a member of the hard right in late middle-age. At this point in the play Jeremy, in his thirties, is a history master at a minor public school. He is speaking to a left-wing schoolboy.

————————————

Jeremy All right, then. Look, I was born in Halifax. And although my family would not have known an opportunist tendency had one leant over and bit them – in fact they thought that reading stunted growth – we all knew people who had elder brothers, fathers, friends, who were either near or in the Party. And some of them, the very best of them, went off to Spain. And the very best of those did not come back.

And so when *we* came of age, when it was all over, the thirties and the war, we had this feeling we were fifteen years too young. And I tell you, there's no stranger feeling than the feeling that instead of being past it, it's past you.

And what we'd missed, of course, was all the glory. And indeed the confidence, that once you'd cracked the shackles of the system, every man indeed would be an Aristotle or a Michelangelo. Because in a way, it had already happened. And it hadn't turned out how we thought it would at all. Oh, it was decent sure, and reasonably caring, in its bureaucratic way. . . . And indeed there was full employment and high wages and although there was still some miserable poverty, there was less of it than there'd ever been before. . . . And, for us, of course, we did particularly well, there were scholarships, and places at the less pretentious Oxbridge colleges, and some of us wrote poetry, and others novels, and some were published, and some not . . .

And we worked on literary magazines, or the Third Programme, or we didn't . . .

But you realize there's something missing. The working class is freer than it's ever been. But somewhere, in the no-man's-land between private affluence and public squalor, somewhere inside the Hoover Automatic or the Mini-Cooper, behind the television or underneath the gramophone, those wonderful possessions . . . you hear a kind of scream. The scream of the possessed.

And you realize there's all the difference in the world, between liberty and liberation.

15

Junk *by John Retallack, adapted from the novel by Melvin Burgess*

Tar is a fourteen-year old runaway, fleeing a physically abusive father and psychologically manipulative mother. He is deeply in love with his girlfriend, Gemma, and unaware that she's less interested in him. At this point Tar is clean of drugs but will soon find himself following Gemma into the drug culture.

At this point Tar has just telephoned Gemma and persuaded her to join him in Bristol.

———————————

Tar (*to audience*) I'd been feeling pretty down, being here in Bristol, sleeping rough, on my own. It was really depressing. But after the call, when I walked away from the phone box, I noticed the dandelions. They'd always been there, but I hadn't noticed them before. It was a solid mass of yellow, bright, golden yellow. Wild dandelions, not put there for me to look at, but there because they wanted to be there. All along the grubby street it was ablaze with yellow and everyone was walking up and down without even noticing them. It sounds stupid, but it was like the flowers had come out for Gemma. I love yellow. It's the colour of sunlight. I stood there staring at them, and I had an idea for a painting. A dandelion – just one huge bright yellow dandelion. It would be a big painting. I'm going to do it and give it to Gemma when she comes. And that big happy moment came swooping down, and I reached up a hand and caught hold of it and off I went. I picked a big bunch of dandelions. I felt great again. (*Beat.*) And *then* it hit me. I had nowhere to live.

The Genius *by Howard Brenton*

Leo is a young mathematician and Nobel Prize-winner. He has found the solution that will lead to the construction of the next generation of atomic bomb. Unable to cope with the enormity of his discovery, he takes a post at an English university and attempts to hide away. One day he meets Gilly, a brilliant young student, who has reached a similar set of conclusions . . . it is to her that he addresses this speech.

Leo I'm cold.

He wanders over to his jacket and puts it on as he speaks.

I did the same work in America. It hit me like it hit you. Pur – it – y. The world in a grain of sand, under your fingernail? I had all that innocence. Arrogance.

A silence.

Then I was on a beach. Californian holiday? Up came an individual and sat down beside me. Blue eyes, the body of a surfer. The Government, Gilly, the Government of A – mer – ik – a. And it began.

Gilly What did?

A silence.

Leo Everything. The threat in a smile. The offer of power. A lead role in a cage.

He puffs his cheeks and blows out.

They wanted the work and they wanted me, for Uncle Sam, the free world, for weapons research, for – a bomb. That's what it means, the tune you and I scrawled out with our ballpens. You describe how something lives and dear old human kind will use your words to kill it.

He shakes his head.

Oh boy, the consequence of describing life is death?

He laughs.

I am not a hero. I am an American boy who wants to get fucked. I was made for fame and sex not paranoia in a lonely room, out of my mind that the 'phone is bugged. So I said – OK, no calculation is pure. Therefore calculate no more. I gave up, Gilly. I closed down. I exiled me into my own head. If you are shit scared of the damage you can do, do nothing, eh?

A silence.

In the end they let me alone. And let me hide, here in England. Then you walked out in the snow one morning.

Sweet Panic *by Stephen Poliakoff*

Leo is the patient of Claire, a child psychologist. He's a
bright but disruptive child and a constant source of worry
to his over-worked, stressed parents. In this speech Claire
impersonates Leo describing his recent holiday with his
parents. (Although this part is played by a woman in the
stage play, a male actor can play it out of context.)

———————————————

Clare (*as Leo*) So – there we are travelling through France. I'm on the back seat and Dad – Dad is going on and on about his work, about whether they're going to OK it – how much he wants it to happen. We're eating all this fucking good food, I don't mind French food, some of my mates mind, but I don't, so we're eating this FANTASTIC food, and Dad doesn't even notice, he's just thinking about his Ready Cooked Meals!

One time we do play a game together, while we're going along . . . Dad's idea of a game, spot the English-made car with a French registration number! Not a great game – a little slow because there's only one every half an hour.

We stay a night in this sort of Holiday Inn, not a proper Holiday Inn.

And Mum insists – she really insists, on DANCING. My dad kind of 'walks' behind her. I'm sitting *watching*, of course. Jesus . . . you should have seen it! She looked so fat . . . gross . . . arms wobbling. No, I'm sorry, that's what she looked like.

Clare *chewing gum for a moment.*

And then in the car the next morning they begin quarrelling about whether they're on the right road. And Mum starts shouting and shrieking, 'I'm map reading – you NEVER believe me about anything, you always think I've got it wrong.' And it's like I'm invisible, on the back seat, like they've completely forgotten there's anybody else in the car. And then Mum, she's shrieking, she reaches down, I promise you and she opens the passenger door while we're going along at sixty miles an hour – she does, only a few inches, but she does. Screaming brakes, emergency stop! Nyeeaaaar, (*Mimics noise.*) yell, yell, yell at each other.

And suddenly it's 'Ssshhh, Leo's there, he's listening' – and then there are these two anxious faces looking at me, my MUM and DAD, you know blinking at me – like, 'you didn't actually hear anything, did you, Leo?'

The Sea *by Edward Bond*

A young man is drowned in a boating accident. His death
affects the lives of not only his best friend and his financée
but the entire closed and suspicious community.

Evens makes a living gathering driftwood by the sea.
Despised and feared by the village as a witch, he is in fact
one of the sanest members of the community. In this
speech he is talking to the best friend of the drowned man
on the morning of the inquest.

———————————

Evens I believe in the rat. What's the worst thing you can imagine? The universe is lived in by things that kill and this has gone on for all time. Sometimes the universe is crowded with killing things. Or at any rate there are great pools of them in space. Perhaps that's so now. At other times it falls out that they've killed everything off, including each other of course, and the universe is almost deserted. But not quite. Somewhere on a star a rat will hide under a stone. It will look out on the broken desert and from time to time it will scatter out to feed on the debris. A shambolling, lolloping great rat – like a fat woman with shopping bags running for a bus. Then it scuttles back to its nest and breeds. Because rats build nests. And in time it will change into things that fly and swim and crawl and run. And one day it will change into the rat catcher. I believe in the rat because he has the seeds of the rat catcher in him. I believe in the rat catcher. I believe in sand and stone and water because the wind stirs them into a dirty sea and it gives birth to living things. The universe lives. It teems with life. Men take themselves to be very strong and cunning. But who can kill space or time or dust? They destroy everything but they only make the materials of life. All destruction is finally petty and in the end life laughs at death.

Imagine Drowning *by Terry Johnson*

A woman visits a guesthouse in Cumbria in search of her husband, David, who has been missing for several days. Although the residents of the guesthouse originally deny any knowledge of David it becomes apparent that he did in fact stay with them for some time. In flashback we see that David is a journalist struggling to find a 'big' story with which to revive his career. It also becomes apparent that David is struggling with several conflicting emotions – not only concern about his job but also his growing hatred for his loving wife.

In this speech David is describing to Tom, a political campaigner, his experiences as a foreign correspondent. He is drunk.

———————————

David When the really bad news began . . . South Africa, 1985, I was there. My first serious foreign assignment. If they'd known how series it was going to get they'd have sent someone older. Someone like Stephenson. He was there; this Fleet Street legend, pissed old cynic, I hated him. When the worst started there were twelve of us in a hotel television lounge sending out the most fantastic stuff. A dozen of us yelling down the only three phone lines. Runners coming in with eye-witnesses. A fourteen-year-old boy dripping blood on my word-processor, I remember, wouldn't go wash up, wanted to tell us, wanted us to tell. The din, the adrenalin. You've never felt anything like it. Then four days later the lines were down, metaphorically I mean. Everything was D notice. It piled up until we stopped collecting. Material that would have made a dozen colour supplements, let alone the actual news, and no way to pass it out without the actual risk of actual arrest, and – we had the evidence – of actual torture. I was desperate to get this stuff out, but after a couple of days the hotel lounge had come to a full stop. All these so called foreign correspondents sitting around drinking iced coffee. Only topic of conversation seemed to be where to get your laundry done. Stephenson sat there. He could see I was furious.

He put down his glass, and said, 'You hear that noise?'

'What noise?'

It was silent as the grave.

I said, 'What noise?'

He looked at the dead typewriters and the comatose phones and he said, 'The silence. Do you know what that silence is?'

I said no.

He said, 'Genocide. The silence is genocide.'

Gosforth's Fête, *(from* Confusions) *by Alan Ayckbourn*

Gosforth, the local publican, is attempting to organize the annual village fête. The odds are stacked against him; the weather is bad, the sound system doesn't work, and the local dignitary who will open the fête has arrived early. Then Gosforth is told that he is about to become a father. . . . Gosforth has just bustled into the tent and is explaining the itinerary to the local celebrity and his companion.

Gosforth We rented both these damn tents, you see. Didn't really open them up until today. Didn't have the space. When we do, we find half the guy ropes are missing off the main marquee – this one's safe enough – had to do an emergency job. Not a window left in the district with any sash cord.

He laughs.

Now, the curriculum goes as follows. Two-thirty p.m. we plan to kick-off. I'll give you a short introduction – needn't be too long – as soon as you've finished – up strikes the band – got them coming over from Hadforth – they should be here – why aren't they? – then if you can mingle about a bit if you don't mind a spot of mingling – have a go at bowling for the pig – just seen Fred Crake's trailer so the pig's arrived safely, thank God – roll a few pennies and all that sort of thing – then, at three-thirty – if you can stay till then – hope you can – Second Little Pendon Wolf Cubs' P.T. Display, organized by Stewart Stokes – that should go on for about half-an-hour – four o'clock tea, courtesy Milly Carter and assorted ladies – four-thirty, soon as they've swallowed their biscuits – novelty races, fathers' race, mothers' race, three-legged grandfathers' race, all that sort of rubbish – five-thirty to six – final round-off with an organized sing-song with the Hadforth Band – has the Reverend managed to get the song-sheets run off? – ten pounds to a quid he hasn't – six o'clock all pack up, dismantle tents – seven-thirty all cleared away because old Swales wants the field back for his cows first thing in the morning. Hope you can stay for a bit of the fun.

Strugglers *by Richard Cameron*

When one of their friends has as epileptic fit and scalds herself, a group of school-leavers with special needs struggle to raise the money to buy her a microwave. The play shows the experiences of the young people as they struggle to come to terms with the harsh world outside their school and still remain true to themselves.

Victor is sixteen years old, friendly and loving and with a tendency to be overly trusting in a cruel world. He has learning difficulties. In this speech he is talking to God having just been bullied by 'normal' boys on the way home from school.

Victor Our Father, who art in heaven, why can't everybody be nice to each other? Them boys were being a bit nasty, weren't they? I'm sorry I swore but at least I never said it out loud, only in my head. You can still hear it, though, can't you? I don't know why I get swearwords in my head. They just seem to get inside. I'm sorry. And I'm sorry about lying as well but when Billy told me about his sister meeting somebody famous off television I just started telling him about Victor Sylvester. I remember my granddad telling me about him.

Rufus *and his cousin appear. They are playing a board game.*

Victor Can I say a prayer for Rufus's mum? She is in hospital. Rufus hasn't told me what's the matter because he doesn't say much but I think she is having a baby but with her being old they keep them in hospital, don't they? He says he likes being with his cousin. She got the 'Game of Life' for Christmas and they play it a lot, he said. I suppose it's good practice for when we all leave school.

Janet *and* **Lyndsay** *appear, in* **Janet***'s house.*

I'm getting a bit worried about leaving now it's getting so near. I hope you'll keep looking after all my friends once we've all left. Even though we won't see each other much I know you'll make sure we're all still thinking about each other. I know it depends on the Prime Minister and not you, but will you try to get us jobs we like doing and meet nice people not nasty like those boys. (*Pause*). Hang on, I think I can hear my mum calling me. I'll be back in a minute. (*Goes off.*)

Rents *by Michael Wilcox*

Rents is a comedy set in Edinburgh which follows the experiences of two rent-boys as they search for security and love.

This speech is taken from the original monologue on which the play was based.

Robert I started hanging around when I was fifteen and once I began to break through I had a crazy time for six months . . . I was astonished at the sort of custom I had with all these men, coming all over me in the most unlikely situations. Christ . . . if a guy took me to the cinema, I'd go out to the bog with him during the advertisements and let him screw me. Never got caught or anything . . . some of the guys that came in must have realised what was going on . . . but they just went blind to the whole business. Anyway . . . I just couldn't stop myself. It wasn't the sex or the pleasure of it exactly . . . it was seeing a grown man that I most likely despised getting that excited about me . . . my body . . . and feeling the tension and the sweat of him when he came . . . and his dejection as he cleaned himself up with bog roll after . . . the fear in his eye. Hatred in me gave me my satisfaction . . . and the power. I knew they were using me and didn't give a shit about me and I wanted to be sure they paid for it one way or another. One man punched me in the mouth when I laughed at him . . . I had more respect for him after that and went with him a few times . . . which was unusual.

For good times I went with young men or lads of my own age . . . the beauty and pain exploding inside me. Christ . . . that's something I've lost now . . . I keep searching.

A State Affair *by Robin Soans*

Paul is a young criminal and drug addict living on an estate in the Buttershaw area of Bradford, 2000.

In **A State Affair**, a theatre company who had originally worked with Andrea Dunbar, a writer who had lived in and written about the area in the 1980s, returned to find out how, and if, anything had changed in eighteen years. What they discovered was a community now riven by drugs and crime. The writer Robin Soans interviewed people from the estate and placed their words in a dramatic context. All the text, however, is non-fiction.

In this speech, Paul, who has already been involved in countless burglaries, violent robberies and drug dealing, describes the death of a friend.

Paul This one time Andy phones me . . . he's rattling, got no money, he says, 'Have you got any stuff?' I'd just had a dig – in my arse which is about the only place I've not been – and all I've got left is the wash – the residue left in the spoon – the shit basically. He says, 'That'll do, I'm coming round.' He hobbles in, puts his stick down, I sucked up the wash into a syringe, and I dig him in the neck. He starts going doolally, shouting all sorts, and hops out . . . out of his mind. I can't follow cos I've got this electronic tag on my leg. Twenty minutes later his mum phones. She's panicking, saying he's gone completely doolally, like he needs help urgently. I thought, 'Fuck it' – and ran out of the house. I found him outside the block of flat where he lived. He's thrown himself on to a metal fence. The spikes have gone through his chest. There's blood coming from his nose and ears. I have to physically lift him off. He's dead.

This is my one and only best mate, and I've killed him. I told the police the first I knew was when his mum phoned for help.

The Conquest of the South Pole *by Manfred Karge*

A group of young friends in a small German town, all of whom are long-term unemployed, seek escape from the boredom and depression of their lives by acting out the story of Amundsen's journey to the South Pole.

Slupianeck has assumed the persona of Amundsen himself, finding it easier to communicate through the success of this man rather than through his own personal feeling of failure. This speech takes place at the end of the play when they have attained the 'Pole'. Slupianeck is told by his friends that they are all either leaving Germany, have found work or are going to the Job Centre to look for work. Slupianek cannot relinquish the fantasy world he has established and compares a visit to the Job Centre with exploring the Antarctic.

———————————

Slupianek What on earth's keeping Bjaaland?

Seiffert is at the Job Centre again. He set off pretty early. He's still bleary-eyed but wide awake and raring to go. The white-washed vestibule. A notice board, rooms, floors, right, left, straight ahead. Go straight ahead. Hold the course. Do I wander off to the right? No. To the left? Don't wander off to the left, you're obsessed by the left, raving leftie. Straight ahead, for ever straight ahead. A block of ice. No, a staircase. To the first floor. Step by step. Watch out, crevasses in the ice. Is there a bridge of snow anywhere? The last step, the first floor. A glass door. A long, grey-black polished corridor. Fluorescent lights on the ceiling. Long wooden benches crammed full of penguins. Nothing but penguins sitting there, keeping quiet, their heads bowed. No space to sit down. Standing room only. Ahead, the door that meant hope. It's white, white. What's behind it? The South Pole. Is that where the Pole actually is?

Really and truly, or only from the plane? Perhaps it's only a wall of ice. Sheer, unclimbable. What am I saying, unclimbable? What are my ice-pick and crampons for? Hacking out steps. Click click. Step by step. Breath comes in spasms. Freezes immediately on your fur and goggles. I can't see a thing any more. But still, on, on. Remove that curtain. It isn't your turn yet, yells a penguin. Paws off that curtain. A penguin leaves. A bit of a bench becomes free. On no account sit down, on no account. If you're sitting down you fall asleep and freeze to death, easy as pie. When's my turn? Be patient, it takes time, please be patient. A pink cloud. I fall asleep. God help me. I fall asleep standing up. How much time has passed? The door is open. Come in. Filing cabinets right and left. Don't lose your way. Straight ahead. Hold the course. Do sit down. No, I won't sit down, says Seiffert. Do you want me to freeze to death? We've got oil-heaters, portable. Would you like a coffee? Yes, coffee, says Seiffert, a gulp of hot coffee. To wash down the lump in my throat. And you are? Bjaaland, says Seiffert. Funny name. We haven't got that in our files. Well than, says Seiffert, Adams. Yes, Adams, says Seiffert, I'm called Adams. Why are you gaping? I, says Seiffert, and you must excuse me, am snowblind. I, says Seiffert, am a moose and snowblind. A snowblind moose. Ponies, says Seiffert, are in any case better than dogs. They have to be shot. Rosi, says Seiffert, got a slip made of seal-skin. I beg you, says Seiffert, on bended knees, for a job on an ice-breaker. On an ice-breaker? No, says Seiffert, with a nice baker. I demand, yells Seiffert, a job with a nice baker. Yes, I am perfectly calm, says Seiffert. Yes, says Seiffert, I will sit down. You've got to telephone, says Seiffert, I understand. Yes, says Seiffert, I understand. Yes, says Seiffert, I quite understand. Any minute now two nice men will appear, because I'm far too cold in this thin jacket, in all this ice and snow. Yes, says Seiffert, they are good friends. They, says Seiffert, have my best interest at heart. Yes, they have a lovely warm jacket for me. But I don't want it, yells Seiffer. What are windows for?

The Children *by Edward Bond*

This is the opening speech in the play. Set in an unspecified future, Joe, is the teenage son of a psychologically disturbed mother. His perceptions of how his behaviour affects his mother are contrary to reality and he blames himself for her strange and erratic behaviour.

In this scene he's crossing the allotments on the way home, talking to a stuffed puppet . . .

Joe Late. Dark soon. This used to be allotments. That's what the little sheds were for. They're falling down. They say they're haunted. Got spiders in them. (*Points.*) Railway line.

Don't cry. Shouldn't have brought you with me today. Brought you because you cried. Now you're crying even more. Are you afraid? You don't like the dark. You'll be all right for one night. Are you hungry? I'll bring you some sweets in the morning. What sweets shall I bring you?

My tea'll be cold. Mum'll be on the warpath. She's waiting to go out. If you could walk we'd go back together. I'd drop you at your front door. Stand out in the street. Hear them shout at you inside for being late. We'd laugh about it in the morning. That used to be my jacket. Passed it on to you when I grew out of it. Still put my things in the pockets. Secret hiding place. Don't cry. If you cry I won't bring you the sweets. Oh dear! – now he'll cry even more. What sweets d'you want? I'll buy them with Mum's fag money. Say I lost it. She won't believe me. I don't care.

Why do I drag you around? You get me into trouble. Didn't go to school today because of you. Mum won't have you in the house any more. She'd send you to the jumble sale. 'That's where you won him in the raffle. Take him back. Make some money out of him.' Or chuck you in the rubbish when I'm at school. You stare at me. If you were real we'd quarrel. That'd be that! I'd tell you to get lost! I even have to do your talking for you. Sometimes I hear myself talk and think it's you. Anyone listening now would think I'm mad. It's got to stop! I'm too old for you! You're nothing! A puppet stuffed with packing! [. . .] I'll have to kill you.

He goes out. He comes back with a brick.

You won't feel it. Cheerio. (*He drops the brick on the puppet's head.*) Shut your eyes. Be dead.

He goes out. He comes back with a brick. He stops, wanders a few steps.

Anything goes wrong in our house Mum hits me. Don't know why. Am I supposed to change the world? (*He goes to the puppet. Looks at it.*) Got dirty green on your face. Off the brick. If I had a torch there'd be blood where I walk between you and the bricks.

He drops the brick on the puppet's head. He goes out and comes back with a brick. He drops it on the puppet's head.

That's enough. Won't leave you here when it's done. Stream at the back. Allotment holders got water from it for their plants. Mucky. Full of crates and trollies. Won't throw you in the water. Lay you on the bank. Out of sight. The cats and dogs won't get you. If you turned into a ghost you'd hear the stream run when it rained. No ghosts. There's nothing like that.

He picks up the puppet. Half-hugs and playfully half-swings it from side to side.

You're nearly dead. One more.

He puts down the puppet. Starts to go. Suddenly stops.

Has to be! (*Runs back to the puppet. Picks up a brick. Hits the puppet with the brick.*) Has to be! Can't give you away to someone who doesn't care! (*Hits the puppet with the brick.*) Can't leave you on a bus! (*Hits the puppet with the brick.*) Someone might find you – who didn't humiliate you! (*Hits the puppet with the brick.*) Didn't hurt you! (*Hits the puppet with the brick.*) I can't! You're mine! (*Pause.*) Phew! (*Stands, Looks at his hand.*) Muck. (*Brushes his hands together.*) Dark. Mum'll rave. She's going out with her new boyfriend.

Barbarians *by Barrie Keeffe*

Barbarians is a trilogy of plays following the experiences of three East End teenagers as they leave school and try to find employment.

Jan has joined the Army and is about to go on a tour of duty in Northern Ireland. Although normally reticent about his past, the night prior to his departure he talks of his mother for the first time.

———————

Jan They laughed at me mum . . . destroyed her. They took away her bowels, to stop it spreading. The doctors did. They gave her a plastic bag, she hated it – the bag to urinate in. She hated it, she said it was like having a bath wearing a life belt. She used to sing in the pub, by the flats. She wanted a garden. We never had one in the flats. Never lived on the ground, me mum didn't. The pub had a garden. Sit there drinking her Dubonnet and lemonade. She used to sing at the pub at nights sometimes. They had turns and she'd get up and sing. Even when she was very ill. And one Saturday night she had this . . . she had this lovely voice, beautiful. When she sang 'Goodnight Irene', old women cried. She was a legend, her voice.

(*He sings.*) Irene, goodnight, Irene goodnight I'll see you in my dreams.

Pause. He begins to cry.

And this Saturday night, they had this dwarf comic. He told tall stories and jokes, made me mum laugh. He said – see, there used to be a lot of blacks in there, and so he told jokes about the blacks. They liked them, I mean – well, they had to like them.

Pause.

And when he went off the stage, they never took off the microphone. And it was still there, only about three and a half feet from the ground. They asked for a song and me Uncle Harold, he said to me mum: 'Give us a song, Elsie. And the other people, they all said: 'Give us a song, Elsie. And she said: 'O no, I can't.' And then they all started chanting: 'Elsie, give us a song.' And the man on the piano, called Charles, he started playing the beginning of 'Goodnight Irene' 'cause it was like her signature tune and eventually she got up and she was very overcome because of all the warmth and the pub was nice, with warmth and friendship. And she stood up and the drummer gave her the hand microphone and still they forgot the dwarf's microphone which was still standing right in front of my mum. And she put up her hand to stop everyone cheering and the piano player asked for hush and my mum said: 'I'm very overcome to know you all cared for me 'cause of the collection from the pub to send me flowers when I had my unfortunate operation . . .' And she was very err . . . moved. Moved. And in the quiet, there was this sound . . . this noise. Coming out of the loudspeakers. Because the dwarf's microphone was still switched on . . . it was standing about waist height to my mother. The sound of gushing water. The microphone picked up the sound of my mum passing water into her plastic bag. Everyone could hear it. Through the loudspeakers, the sound went on and some people they . . . they . . .

Pause.

And some people, some of the people . . .

Pause.

Laughed. They laughed.

He stops crying. Long silence.

That night at home, she got up out of bed and went to the bathroom and drank a pint of bleach. Which killed her.

Pause.

After that, it was very quiet at home. I went two nights every week to the Cadets and then . . . I signed up. I don't . . . talk about it much. When I had the medical, I didn't tell them about my mum . . . I thought it best to say 'natural causes'.

Have I None *by Edward Bond*

Set in an unspecified future time, Jams is some form of
security/police officer, patrolling the streets of a ruined part
of the city. He returns home to tell his wife, Sara, of his
strange meeting with an old lady.

———————————

Jams   Guess what happened on patrol today. Things people get up
to! We were in the old town. Part they cleared years ago. Bandits
hide up there sometimes. We saw an old woman walking on the
street ahead of us. Told the driver to slow down. Guess what she was
carrying [. . .] Carrying it under her arm. Picture! [. . .] She turns off
on this track. Side road once. Lepal Street – sign still up. She goes
through a door. Told the driver to drive past. Looked through the
holes in the wall. Vanished. Stopped the truck. Went back with
Dinny. Crep' in the doorway. The old biddy's inside. Picture stood
on the rubble by the wall. She's grubbing about in the dirt. What's
she lost? You listening to me? (*No reaction.*) A nail! She's looking for
a nail. [. . .] The old biddy's found a table. Dragging it over the
rubble – hard work I can tell you! – it's bucking about like a calf
being dragged to the butchers! Coat and blouse hanging undone.
Hate slovenliness! Catches her hem in her heel. Rip. What a mess!
[. . .] The table's there – eventually. Climbs on. Bangs the nail in the
wall with a brick. Brick breaks. Scrapes the skin off her fingers.
Blood. Looks round for the picture. It's left on the pile by the wall. I
go in. Hang the picture on the wall. See her close up. Long white
eyebrows hanging in her eyes like dead spiders. She starts to pee
herself. Trickles down on the table. Runs her hand through her hair.
Leaves a read streak on the grey. Chriss she'll stink the cab out! I'm
sitting up front with the driver! She never looked at the picture.
Weren't even straight. Sea. Forest – mountains behind. The table's
like a butcher's block: blood, piss. She's stood on the edge. Rocks –

the leg's skewing off. Can't give her a hand, can't touch anything like that. She comes down – jumps or topples – skins her shins. Screeches like a nail skidding down a glass runway. Chriss I'm definitely sitting in front! – blood – piss – now hollering! She didn't though. Just gurgles with the snot up her snout. That dick Johannson's still in the gap. Stayed when I sent 'em back. I beckoned him with one finger – and point down to the bitch on the bricks. Not a dicky-bird – did it by pointing. That narked him. He had to drag her to the vehicle. We drove her to the centre. They won't feed her. Her age, why prolong the misery? We played football with the picture. Kicked it under the rubble – where the CO can't see it if he comes snooping. They cleared those houses since thirty years back. They weren't allowed to take their old stuff with them. Where's she hid a picture all them years? (*Shrugs.*) Probably weren't hers. Found it on a dump. Not her house. All look the same when they're knocked down. Not even her street.

Rat in The Skull *by Ron Hutchinson*

Rat in The Skull is set in a Paddington police station where a suspected Irish terrorist is held awaiting interrogation by an RUC officer. The play shows the distrust and dislike both between the two Irishmen and the British police of whom they are both 'guests'. The terrorist addresses this speech to the audience whilst alone in his cell.

Roche Not a hand on me. The next two days, not a hand on me. They must have been running buses, there was coppers coming in from all over the place. I swear to God, there was even a couple who said would I mind if they got married in the cell, they were that proud of me. Or proud of having me, more than like, Michael Patrick de Valera Demon Bomber Roche. I said no. You like your privacy. Not that there was too much of that, with the formation teams of interrogators coming in every hour, on the hour: hard man; soft man; 'Like a smack in the gob?'; 'Like a fag or a woman?'; relays and queues of the bastards, and as one falls dead with exhaustion it's out by the legs, and the next man, please. And the barking at you, and the showing you snaps of bits and pieces of what was left when the thing went up, and being told they'd stuff you in a bin-sack and have you out of the chopper if it was up to them, and hanging's too good, and the light left on all the time, and the peering up your backside with the nightlight, and breakfast a mug of cold tea the copper said he'd gobbed in, and every time you were left alone whoever walked by the cell door felt he had to aim a kick at it; just to say hallo—

Well I wouldn't have minded so much, but I was nothing like the photy-fits.

I'm no oil-painting, God knows, and that was the case even before I had the nose, lip and eye job done, but fair play, it was nothing like. It was nothing like and I was saying nothing, and were they as pissed-off a bunch of cops as ever knew they'd only the forensic to go on, and though that was going to be enough they'd feel safer with a cough or more. But still never a hand on me. And fair play, the Mick was being stitched all ways up, by the book and down the line and not a foot put wrong and I'm telling you there were twenty-five big ones coming up, sure fire thing, the world was turning into iron bars for yours truly Michael Patrick de Valera You-Know-The-Rest-Of-It Roche. Banged-up, closed-down, one stitched Mick.

Beached *by Kevin Hood*

Pete, a handsome but dumb teenager, has run away with Maria, an ex-schoolfriend. Pete has attacked Maria's father during a bungled burglary attempt and may well have accidentally murdered him. The teenagers are both spending the night on the beach in a bird sanctuary. For both of them this is proving to be a night of bleakness as they both face the realisation that the reality of their lives is not as rosy as their daydreams.

As Maria settles down for the night Pete recalls the time he visited the sanctuary on a school trip.

Pete I like the dark, always 'ave.

Pete *discovers that* **Maria** *has set up on her own. He lays out the sleeping bag on the other side of the rucksack.* **Maria** *puts out her cigarette and lies down.*

Used to get in the corner under my bed for hours, with the cat, and nobody'd know I was there. Dark does somethin' to the sound – the walls was thin in our house. That school trip . . .

Pete *gets into the sleeping bag, leans out and unpacks rucksack, coffee mugs out, water in an old lemonade bottle, camping stove.*

Pete That power station, this big building and these engine things, fuckin' enormous. These . . . things big as buses and vibratin'. (*Pause.*) No, not 'avin' that, I thought. So I fucked off. Turned round and fucked off. I went straight through the door, through the gate, and this fat ol' cunt of a teacher come runnin' after. 'Where you going?' he goes. 'Where d'you think you're goin'?' Used to play for Millwall or somethin', 'e did. Years ago, though – 'cos I left 'im on 'is 'ands and knees in the sand coughin' 'is lungs out. No chance. 'I'll 'ave you for this,' he goes, but I just ran and ran. Till I come 'ere. (*Beat.*) And then I stopped. (*Pause.*) Me 'ands is shakin'. Look at 'em. Maria?

Maria *is alseep.*

I wouldn't go back for nothing. I was scared shitless. 'I'll 'ave you for this.' (*Pause.*) And 'e did. They always do if you go back. (*Pause.*)

The Fire Raisers *by Max Frisch*

Two arsonists move into a man's house and begin their preparations to raze it to the ground. The nearer they come to lighting the fire the more he attempts to befriend and placate them.

Beelzebub is revealed to be one of the fire raisers in the afterpiece when the man and his wife find themselves in heaven.

Beelzebub My childhood faith! My childhood faith!

Thou shalt not kill, ha, and I believed it.

What are they making of my childhood faith!

The Figure *cleans his finger nails.*

I, the son of a charcoal burner and a gypsy woman, who couldn't read but knew the Ten Commandments off by heart, I'm possessed by the Devil. Why? Simply because I scorned all commandments. Go to hell, Joe, you're possessed by the Devil everyone said to me, and I went to hell. I lied, because then everything went better, and I became possessed by the Devil. I stole whatever took my fancy and became possessed by the Devil. I whored with whatever came my way, married or unmarried, because I had the urge to, and I felt fine when I gave way to my urge and became possessed by the Devil.

And they fear me in every village, for I was stronger than all of them, because I was possessed by the Devil. I tripped them up on their way to church, because I felt the urge, I set fire to their stables while they were praying and singing, every Sunday, because I felt the urge, and I laughed at their God who did not lay hold of me. Who felled the fir tree that killed my father in broad daylight? And my mother, who prayed for me, died of worry over me, and I entered the orphanage to set fire to it, and the circus to set fire to it, because I felt the urge more and more, and I started fires in every town simply in order to be possessed by the Devil. – Thou shalt! Thou shalt not! Thou shalt! Because we had no newspapers and no radio out there in the forest, we had only a Bible, and therefore I believed that one became possessed by the Devil if one killed and ravished and murdered and mocked every commandment and destroyed whole cities – that's what I believed! . . .

The Figure *laughs.*

It's no laughing matter, Willie!

The Pitchfork Disney *by Philip Ridley*

Presley shares a home with his 'twin' sister Hayley. Both of them are reclusive. Following the supposed death of their parents the siblings have stayed at home, only venturing out at night and living on chocolate bars. They tell each other stories about their childhood, reminiscing about their early relationship with their parents.

In this speech Presley reminds Hayley of the only time his mother raised a hand to him.

Presley I saved my pocket money for three weeks. I didn't buy anything. No comics, no crisps, no sweets. I went to a pet shop and bought this tiny green snake instead. A grass snake they called it. When I got home I played with the snake. It felt warm and soft. I was scared but I still had to hold it. I liked the way it wrapped itself round my fingers like an electric shoelace. And then . . . then I realised. I could never keep it. Not as a pet. Where would it sleep? What would it eat? Where would it go when I went to school? It was a stupid thing to buy. So I had to get rid of it. But how? All sorts of things occurred to me: flush it down the toilet, bury it, throw it from a tower block. But all the while another thought was taking shape. A thought so wonderful it seemed the only thing to do. So I got a frying pan and put it on the gas stove. I put a bit of butter in the pan and turned the gas up full. The fat started to crackle and smoke. I dropped the snake into the frying pan. It span round and round and its skin burst open like the skin of a sausage. It took ages to die. Its tiny mouth opened and closed and its black eyes exploded. But it was wonderful to watch. All that burning and scalding and peeling. I got a fork and stuck the prongs into its skin. Boiling black blood bubbled out of the holes. When the snake was dead I put it on a plate. I cut the snake into bite size pieces. I tasted it. Like greasy chicken. I ate it all and licked the plate afterwards. When Mummy got home she saw I'd been cooking and hit me. She didn't know anything about the snake. All she was worried about was the scorched patch on the frying pan. She said, 'I'll have to buy a new one now.' But she never did. (*Rushes to the kitchen and returns with the scorched frying pan.*) Look!

One for the Road *by Willy Russell*

It is Dennis's fortieth birthday. As his guests arrive, discussing the neighbourhood community programme and the mysterious attacks on garden gnomes, Dennis struggles to break out of his domesticity and find a new meaning to his life. Here he is talking to his friends after his birthday dinner about his pet dislikes.

Dennis Every time I see a new piece of Tupperware in the house it feels like another little invasion has taken place . . . It seems to have a will of its own. I dreamt about it the other night. I dreamed that all the Tupperware in the house gelled together into one big plastic mass and began rollin' and slidin' up the stairs, on and on, through the bedroom door and sliding across the carpet, creepin' up onto the bed and pouncin' on me. The more I struggled, the more wrapped up in it I became until finally I stopped struggling and became The Tupperware Man. (. . .)

An' in the next part of the dream I was Tupperware Man himself – I could fly and everything I touched turned to Tupperware. The world was in a panic. They sent Superman after me, and Batman and Robin and Luke Skywalker and Wonder Woman. But they were all helpless in the face of Tupperware Man. I turned them all into Tupperware – Batman and Robin became a butterdish an' egg cup, Superman was turned into a picnic box, Luke Skywalker into a salad spinner an' I turned Wonder Woman into a huge, tit-shaped jelly mould. Planet Earth was in danger of becoming a Tupperware Globe when the Americans came up with a new invention – Tupperware Woman. They sent her after me and I tried to resist, but it was no good, I was helpless in the face of her. An irresistible force drew me towards her, I couldn't stop myself, I struggled to keep away from her but I was drawn on and on. Beaten, I gave up, I kissed her and me lid flew off. It was all over.

The Hunt for Red Willie *by Ken Bourke*

Donegal, 1820s. A local magistrate is killed and rumour spreads that it is the infamous Red Willie. Red Willie is actually a mask and legend has it that it is cursed and can turn the wearer to evil deeds. Fardy McHugh, a young peasant and maker of the illegal poitin, is suspected of being Red Willie. He goes on the run, determined to find the real murderer and clear his name.

In the following speech Fardy is hiding in the forest. His only companion is the Red Willie mask. He talks to it, reminiscing about his childhood.

––––––––––––––––––

Fardy I remember the first time he took me out on the lake: there was an old boat here, and he lifted a pair of oars out of somewhere, and out we went on to the water, gliding away like a big dirty swan. And I said to him, 'Daddy, why is there water in the bottom of the boat?' and he smiled and he said, 'That'll be the rain that's after gathering in it.' And I thought, 'My daddy knows everything.' And the sun never shone so bright as it did that day. And then I asked him, 'Why is it bubbling up like that, Daddy?' and he stopped rowing, and looked down into the bottom of the boat, and he scratched his chin, and he said, 'There's a fecking hole in it, son. We may turn back.' So back we rowed, and the water was rising up inside the boat and I was scooping out bits of it with my cap the best I could, until he decided it was time to abandon ship, and he hopped over the side, and the water was up to his chin, and I remember thinking his head was going to float away on its own, then he took me on to his shoulders like he was St Christopher, and he carried me on to the shore.

Spell #7 *by Ntozake Shange*

Spell #7 is written as a poetic piece reflecting the lives and experiences of black people in America. A group of performers meet in a bar to sing, dance and talk about their lives.

Eli is the bartender who listens to their problems. He is also a poet. In this speech he has just broken up a fight between two female dancers.

---

eli people keep tellin me to put my feet on the ground
i get mad & scream/ there is no ground
only shit pieces from dogs horses & men who dont live
anywhere/ they tell me think straight & make myself
somethin/ i shout & sigh/ i am a poet/ i write poems
i make words cartwheel & somersault down pages
outta my mouth come visions distilled like bootleg
whiskey/ i am like a radio but i am a channel of my own
i keep sayin i write poems/ & people keep askin me
what do i do/ what in the hell is going on?
people keep tellin me there are hard times/ what are
you gonna be doin ten years from now/
what in the hell do you think/ i am gonna be writin poems
i will have poems inchin up the walls of the lincoln tunnel/
i am gonna feed my children poems on rye bread with horseradish/
i am gonna send my mailman off with a poem for his wagon/
give my doctor a poem for his heart/ i am a poet/
i am not a part-time poet/ i am not a amateur poet/
i don't even know what that person cd be/ whoever that is
authorizing poetry as an avocation/ is a fraud/
put yr own feet on the ground

An Experienced Woman Gives Advice *by* *Iain Heggie*

Kenny is the younger lover of Bella, his college professor. Kenny and Bella's relationship is starting to fracture as Kenny graduates. He is eager to move down to London but is caught between both love and guilt over Bella.

In the following speech Kenny has been unfaithful to Bella with another young student, Nancy. Bella has discovered this infidelity but hasn't yet spoken to Kenny about it. Kenny, realising that his secret might be discovered, decides to spill the beans to Bella.

Kenny That's why I'm going to tell you what happened last night. The whole truth this time. The trivial truth. You'll laugh when you hear. [. . .] All Stick's pals did was take me out for a drink. I didn't like Stick's pals. I didn't know what it was I didn't like. I was *trying* to like them. So I took a drink. I still didn't like them. I took another. They were still pigs. Then another. Scum. Another. Another. Another. No change. And all this time pub to pub to . . . night-club. This girl comes up. You wouldn't believe it. Up she came. And she's talk talk talk and says: 'I'm short, stupid and fat. What do you see in me?' I say: 'No you're not.' She says: 'So you fancy me than?' If that's not enough next it's 'Dance?' 'No.' 'Dance.' 'No thanks.' 'Dance or I'll scream.' 'All right.' So dance, dance, dance again. Next thing: past all her pals. Past her pals, we're walking. Hand in hand. Waves at them. She *waves* at them. *I've* to wave at them. Outside we'll split up. I'm thinking: 'If I can just get outside with her we'll split up. She'll let me go. She'll have had what she wanted. Her friends seeing her getting picked up.' So outside, I say: 'Been nice. I'm off home now. Cheerio.' What did that start? '*You* misled me. *You* promised me you'd take me home. *You* took me away from my friends. *You* raped me.' And screaming. She started screaming. She/ A taxi. I jumped in to a taxi. I was making a run for it. She got in with me. 'Get out.' 'No.' 'Please get out.' 'No.' 'Get out or I'll get out.' 'Drive, driver.' 'Where to?' (He goes.) She goes: 'Just drive.' He drives, but keeps asking for an address. I don't know why I did it. I should have given a false address. I must've thought the driver would *know* I'd given a false address. You won't believe it, Bella: I gave the driver *Stick's* address. But then I thought: Yes! Why not take her back to Stick's. Take her back, *sober her up* at Stick's, send her home. Up the stairs. In. she wants a drink. Another drink. Music she wants. Louder. Louder. Louder. Another drink. Then the doorbell goes. I thought: 'A neighbour come to complain about the music.' No. This guy standing there. Says to call him Irving. Friend of Stick. (He says.) I didn't want to let him in. So I'm holding him there, holding him there. But what if he *is* a friend of Stick? . . . Then I thought: 'Why don't I bring him in? Use him somehow to get rid of the girl.' In he comes. Nancy meet Irving. Irving meet Nancy. By this time Nancy's *really* drunk and all over both of us. I thought: 'Leave them to it.' Then I thought: 'I can't. He'll take advantage.' So I show him to his bedroom! He comes with me. But shouting, bawling. Something about he'd travelled from London specially. I've spoilt his night. I've spoilt his weekend. I've spoilt *his life*. I'm only doing it because I want the girl to myself. Wait till Stick hears. When I get back to Nancy, she/ she/ well, she was actually *asleep*, Bella.

The Accrington Pals *by Peter Whelan*

The Accrington Pals are a battalion of men from Lancashire who are going over to fight in the trenches in the First World War.

Ralph has a carefree, expansive nature and rarely seems to take the war seriously. He is involved with Eva, a young woman whom he has left behind in Accrington. This is the letter he will never write to Eva; he is in the middle of a battle and knows his death is imminent.

Ralph Oh my dearest, my own little pocket Venus . . . my rose of
Clayton-le-Moors. This is no letter you'll ever get. My love. Sweet
Eva. It's come. After God's long ages it's come and we're up to the
line for the big push. But for the moment we're lost, as ever. Lost
three times finding support trench. Now lost again. It's like a bake
oven this summer night. I'm in a muck sweat. My sore throat's back.
I've spewed my ring up twice. They say Jerry's beat but there's lads
seen his observer balloons up all afternoon watching every move we
made. I was ready enough once. Christmas when they sent us off to
fuckin Egypt to fight Johnnie Turk. But he was whipped before we
got there so I'd got myself ready for nowt. I was ready when they
brought us back and into France. But it's been up and down, round
and round, in and out, waiting and waiting till I don't know how I
shall go at it. I've heard the flies buzzing out there. Every shell or
bombs as falls short sends up clouds. Still, they're only old regulars
lying out there, who, as May would say, are very low at the best of
times. I've been a bastard to you Eva, if you only knew. Slept with
whores. And one little mam'selle in Amiens who'd take no pay. I sat
on her doorstep right after and cried for you. All I want to volunteer
for now is a night raid on your bosom in a field of snowy white
bedsheets. That's a fact.

Foley *by Michael West*

Foley is the disowned son of an Irish gentleman farmer. He has returned to the family home, Castleowen, to take one last look. Foley doesn't regret the loss of the home but feels a sense of grief at his lost relationship with his parents from whom he has been estranged for some time.

The play is a one man show. This speech is early in the play when Foley sets the scene for the first time, explaining to the audience his mixed emotions about his dead parent.

───────────────

Foley My father. Yes.

My father's two grand passions were his land and his beloved funerals. Although he attended the latter with a diligence all too often absent from his labours with the former. The former. That sounds like a bad accent.

You couldn't quite call him a farmer. At least it conjures up the wrong image in my mind. No.

Gentleman farmer. It's a ridiculous phrase, but it does at least convey something of his inherent contradictions and aspirations.

He loved Castleowen, but I think he expected the fields to farm themselves, in a polite and orderly fashion, according to his inconstant whim.

He used to attribute to the land a form of primitive intelligence, an earthy wit, if you like. I can hear him still – 'To keep land you must enter into a dialogue with the forces of nature, a conversation. You can no more force it to your bidding than you can gravity or magnetism. You may as well try and float the apples back into the trees.' He would survey his fields and inform anyone listening. 'The land knows what it wants.'

The land knows what it wants. My god, then it had very low expectations. Merely to thwart my father was sufficient. Funny, I don't know why it and I weren't better acquainted. We had that in common at least.

Serious Money *by Caryl Churchill*

The 'serious money' of the title refers to the fortunes to be made and lost working in the City on the Stock Exchange.

Zac is an American dealer working in Britain. He becomes involved in helping Scilla, another dealer, find the murderer of her brother but his motives are financial rather than compassionate. The play is written as a modern verse play in which every character's over-riding passion is for money.

Zac And the guy walked.
(He walked with twenty million dollars but he walked.)

The financial world won't be the same again
Because the traders are coming down the fast lane.
They don't even know it themselves, they're into fucking or getting
a Porsche, getting a Porsche *and* a Mercedes Benz.
But you can't drive two cars at once.
If you're making the firm ten million you want a piece of the action.
You know you've got it made the day you're offered stock options.
There are guys that blow out, sure, stick too much whitener up their
nose.
Guy over forty's got any sense he takes his golden handshake and
goes.
Because the new guys are hungrier and hornier,
They're Jews from the Bronx and spivs from South Carolina.
It's like Darwin says, survival of the fit,

Now, here in England, it's just beginning to hit.

The British Empire was a cartel.
England could buy whatever it wanted cheap
And make a profit on what it made to sell.
The empire's gone but the City of London keeps
On running like a cartoon cat off a cliff – bang.
That's your Big Bang.
End of the City cartel.
Swell.
England's been fucking the world with interest but now it's a
    different scene.
I don't mind bending over and greasing my ass but I sure ain't using
    my own vaseline.

Now as a place to live, England's swell
Tokyo treats me like a slave, New York tries to kill me, Hong Kong
I have to turn a blind eye to the suffering and I feel wrong.
London, I go to the theatre, I don't get mugged, I have classy friends,
And I go see them in the country at the weekends.

The Age of Consent *by Peter Morris*

Timmy is nineteen years old and a child-killer. Even more horrific, in society's eyes, he killed a small child while only ten years old himself. He's been in prison and remand centres for ten years and is shortly to be released.

In the following monologue he talks about the therapy he has undergone to try and understand his motives for the murder. He describes, for the first time, the actual murder of the small child . . .

———————————

Timmy They made me act it out, they made me think how he felt, what it was like, what I did, how she felt when she couldn't find him . . . what she screamed like . . .

If I've got an imagination at least they me use it till I sweat and use it for the right things now.

But actually . . . doing it . . .

It was just . . . nothing really.

It was . . .

It was interesting. I guess.

Sometimes you see something and it just, it might be wrong, it might be flashy, it might just make no sense but you just have to . . . look . . . like fireworks, or Torvill and Dean, or just the colours in a puddle where there's petrol spilt . . . and you just *look*.

I don't know if I knew what it was . . . they . . .

Like when a toy stops going.

He just . . .

Broken.

He stopped making noise. He stopped moving.

And it was like something was gone.

And I took the battery, it's not what they said, I just . . .

I put it in his mouth, that's where I put it.

Because I thought maybe he'd come back . . . come back on, he'd start moving.

It wasn't dirty . . . it was just . . .

And that's when she was wandering around, screaming, while we were doing that.

And I know what she must've sounded like, looked like . . .

Terrible.

She wasn't beautiful the way a mum should be, I ruined her, I put her there.

But we're both paying for the same five minutes for the rest of our lives.

Me, because of what I did, and I don't know why. You got to believe that, I don't know why I did it, honest.

But her because she turned away for five minutes, to – what? Look at something? Shoplift? Buy some iced buns at the baker's? It doesn't matter what it was, even just for five minutes, no excuse will ever be good enough, for the rest of her life she'll be going back over that, thinking, food, you need food to go on, I was only getting food, for me, for him, and I never want to taste a single thing in my mouth again, I don't want to go on, but I have to, I have to . . .

It won't ever stop. For either of us.

In High Germany *by Dermot Bolger*

Eoin, an Ireland football fan, is waiting at a deserted train station for a train home, after a football match between Ireland and Holland.

In the following speech he describes the journey to the stadium earlier in the day when he and a carriage full of Ireland fans meet a large group of Dutch skinheads . . .

Eoin We boarded one, up in the concrete plaza where we'd been drinking the local beer, around fifty of us, packed in, and took off for the stadium. The first stop was grand, no one on, no one off. The second stop was the problem. There was about sixty of them . . . Dutch skinheads . . . the real McCoy – not the fey little farts of students we'd see in Amsterdam, all Auschwitz pyjamas and haircuts to cure headlice – these boys were mean bastards. Shaven heads painted orange, boots thicker than the walls of Limerick jail, sticks in their hands, eyes like boiled sweets from Bray that would break your teeth.

They didn't all pack on – just as many as would fit between us and the roof. One of them had his face pressed against mine. I could smell the drink as I looked at him and swallowed, then . . .

He lifts his fist.

. . . did what every decent Irishman does when in doubt abroad . . . raised my fist in the air and slagged the Brits.

He thumps his fist off an imaginary ceiling and sings.

'If you hate the Queen of England clap your hands,
If you hate the Queen of England clap your hands . . .'

He lowers his fist and looks at audience.

The Dutch fuckers smiled, banged their sticks against the ceiling and sang. Would we ever get to the stadium? The train stopping and starting, nobody getting on or off, every Irishman racking his brains.

He raises fist and sings frantically.

'Adversane England, Adversane England,
Adversane, Adversane, Adversane England . . .'

He circles the space where the Dutch skinhead would be, and hisses urgently.

Smile, you shagging Dutch bastards, smile.

(*He sings.*)
'The Queen Mother is a man, do-da, do-da . . .'

(*Dutch accent.*) 'Ya, dodadoda!'

He presses himself up as though squeezed against somebody.

The Dutch skinner pressed against me produces a roll-up and gestures with his hand.

He raises two fingers to his lips and shouts.

'Fur!' I didn't need Shane to translate that. I reached in, took a lighter from my pocket and began to raise it.

He reaches into his pocket and takes out a lighter which he holds up. We cannot see if there is anything printed on it or not.

Then I remembered. I'd two lighters. A plain white one and one I'd picked up in some bar in Stuttgart . . . embossed with a Union Jack. I closed my eyes, held it up and flicked it.

He holds his head sideways, grimacing in expectation of the blow as he flicks. He waits a second before cautiously opening his eyes and glancing at the lighter in his hand.

No thump came. I opened my eyes, the lighter was virginal white. And they say there's no God, eh.

Teendreams *by David Edgar and Susan Todd*

Teendreams follows the lives of two women, showing how their teenage idealism of the sixties is eroded by the experiences of being a wife, mother and teacher in the seventies.

Kevin is in his early twenties. He is acting as best man at the wedding of Howard and Rosie; this is his best man speech.

———————————

Kevin Right. Oh, first of all, it falls on me, on your behalf, to express our thanks to the bridesmaids and the pageboy. That's the bridesmaids there, and the pageboy there. Luckily it's quite easy to tell them apart. Usually nowadays to tell the boys from the girls you need a search warrant. But, uh . . . Anyway.

Oh, darlings, I don't know which of you got the bouquet, but could you hand it in, 'cos the man with the window box next door is screaming for it back.

Well, all I can say is, if I've got the right joke here, yes, all I can say is it's a good thing it's not a Scottish wedding. I mean, I went to one last week, and it's the only wedding I been to where the confetti's on elastic.

Anyway, the happy couple. Well, I known 'em, haven't I? Known Howard since he was that high (*very low*). Last Thursday, and Rosie since she was that high (*rather high*). And I know Howard's always wanted someone to look up to . . . not to mention Rosie wanting someone to look down on . . .

Sorry, How, Rosie, had to slip that one in, as the Art Mistress said to the Gardener, sorry, the other way round . . .

Please yourselves.

Well, anyway, I s'pose I better, enough of this merry badinage . . . the first uh, telegram. . . . To Howard and Rosemary, first telegram:

'Note Merged Accounts Stop Future Products Filed In Pending Query Hope Not Triplicate Congrats From All At Office.'

Well, now i'n't that nice. The second telegram, from Frances, 'Don't', I s'pose that's 'Don't . . . forget your promises love Frances', dunno quite what that means, Rosie? Eh? The third—

Blackout on Kevin.

Pond Life *by Richard Cameron*

Trevor is twenty-three and unemployed. He spends his time fishing and making tapes for his friend, Pogo, a mentally ill girl. Trevor's brother has seen a giant carp in the pond and everyone is eager to catch it.

In this scene Trevor and Pogo are talking about the carp and the fishing trip they have planned for that evening. Trevor describes to Pogo the ideal fishing conditions . . .

———————————

Trev I don't know. Some of the best times are heavy rain and thunderstorms. I've sat at night in thunderstorms and it's brought the fish on to feed like mad. I've had a net full by the time the storm has died away. [. . .] Lucky floats. No. Not lucky. Just good to have around. Old friends. Delicate little floats. I look at them sometimes and I can see all the days we've had, sunrises and sunsets on the water. Precious. I can remember the first float my dad gave me. I was about ten. One shift he came home from the pit, didn't come in the house, came straight in here, picked up his rod and tackle bag and went out again. Not a word. Hours later my mam sent me down to the pond to fetch him home. I found him hunched over the rod, the little orange float out on the water in the darkness. There'd been an accident. One of his pals. He couldn't get to him. I didn't know what to say so I said supper was on the table. When he reeled in and lifted the rod there was no hook on the line, no bait. He'd been sat watching a float that was never going to move. I never said anything. I've still got that float. I never use it but it's always in my box. It's not there for catching fish.

Woza Albert *by Mtwa/Ngema/Simon*

Woza Albert attempts to show one particular view of what would happen if Christ came to South Africa. It is a two-hander in which each actor plays a variety of parts ranging from brick makers to the white President of South Africa. At this point Mbongeni is playing an old man being interviewed for the television cameras. Morena is Jesus.

———————————

Mbongeni (*speaking*) Eh? What would happen to Morena if he comes to South Africa? What would happen to Morena is what happened to Piet Retief! Do you know Piet Retief? The big leader of the white men long ago, the leader of the Afrikaners! Ja! He visited Dingane, the great king of the Zulus! When Piet Retief came to Dingane, Dingane was sitting in his camp with all his men. And he thought, 'Hey, these white men with their guns are wizards. They are dangerous!' But he welcomed them with a big smile. He said, he said, 'Hello. Just leave your guns outside and come inside and eat meat and drink beer.' Eeeeii! That is what will happen to Morena today! The Prime Minister will say, just leave your angels outside and the power of your father outside and come inside and enjoy the fruits of apartheid. And then, what will happen to Morena is what happened to Piet Retief when he got inside. Dingane was sitting with all his men in his camp, when Piet Retief came inside. All the Zulus were singing and dancing . . .

Bamya-lo-Kandaba payimpi . . .

Repeats snatches of the song.

And all the time Dingane's men were singing and dancing,

Proudly.

they were waiting for the signal from their kind. And Dingane just stood up . . . He spit on the ground. He hit his beshu and he shouted, Bulalan 'abathakathi. Kill the wizards! Kill the wizards! Kill the wizards! And Dingane's men came with all their spears.

Mimes throat-slitting, throwing of bodies.

Suka! That is what will happen to Morena here in South Africa. Morena here?

Disgusted.

Eeii! Suka!

The Beauty Queen of Leenane *by Martin McDonagh*

Pato is an Irish labourer seeking to escape the repressive society of his small town, Leenane. He has come to England to work on a building site and now has plans to move on to America.

In this speech he recites a letter he's sent to his lover, Maureen, still living in Leenane.

Pato Well, Maureen, I am 'beating around the bush' as they say, because it is you and me I do want to be talking about, if there is such a thing now as 'you and me', I don't know the state of play. What I thought I thought we were getting on royally, at the goodbye to the Yanks and the part after when we did talk and went to yours. And I *did* think you were a beauty queen and I *do* think, and it wasn't anything to do with that at all or with you at all, I think you thought it was. All it was, it has happened to me a couple of times before when I've had a drink taken and was nothing to do with did I want to. I would have been honoured to be the first one you chose, and flattered, and the thing that I'm saying, I was honoured then and I am still honoured, and just because it was not to be that night, does it mean it is not to be ever? I don't see why it should, and I don't see why you was so angry when you was so nice to me when it happened. I think you thought I looked at you differently when your breakdown business came up, when I didn't look at you differently at all, or the thing I said 'Put on your clothes, it's cold', when you seemed to think I did not want to be looking at you in your bra and slip there, when nothing could be further from the truth, because if truth be told I could have looked at you in your bra and slip until the cows came home. I could never get my fill of looking at you in your bra and slip, and some day, God willing, I

74

will be looking at you in your bra and slip again. Which leads me on to my other thing, unless you still haven't forgiven me, in which case we should just forget about it and part as friends, but if you *have* forgiven me it leads me on to my other thing which I was lying to you before when I said I had no news because I do have news. What the news is I have been in touch with me uncle in Boston and the incident with the Wexford man with the bricks was just the final straw. You'd be lucky to get away with your life the building sites in England, let alone the bad money and the 'You oul Irish this-and-that', and I have been in touch with me uncle in Boston and a job he has offered me there, and I am going to take him up on it. Back in Leenane two weeks tomorrow I'll be, to collect up my stuff and I suppose a bit of a do they'll throw me, and the thing I want to say to you is do you want to come with me? Not straight away of course, I know, because you would have things to clear up, but after a month or two I'm saying, but maybe you haven't forgiven me at all and it's being a fool I'm being.

Bloody Poetry *by Howard Brenton*

Bloody Poetry follows the lives of the poets Byron and Shelley over three summers in the early nineteenth century. The poets travel through Europe, writing, arguing and making love with their wives and mistresses.

Polidori is Byron's personal physician. He feels himself to be an object of scorn and amusement to the two couples and resents them bitterly.

Polidori I entered the drawing-room of the Villa Diodati. Outside, there raged the storm. No. Outside the storm raged. No. Outside, the storm abated. No. Outside, the storm I had just left, rolled around the gloomy house. No. No. I was wet and miserable.

He looks around the group. **Byron** *and* **Claire** *kiss passionately.* **Mary** *shifts towards* **Bysshe**, *turning the pages of the Wordsworth. They do not respond to* **Polidori**'s *presence.*

In a flash I saw them, a flash of lightning. The air in the room was heavy with their illicit sexuality, they had been at it, I knew it! I knew it! I knew it! They had thrown their clothes back on, the minute I came to the door! No. The two great poets, were, I observed in contemplation, the women observing a discreet silence.

Mary *turns, she and* **Bysshe** *kiss passionately.* **Polidori** *flinches.*

No. The profligate would-be-poets and their, their whores, lounged upon the floor, and felt disgraced at my entrance, for I brought with me the wind and the rain.

He looks from couple to couple.

No. I am so lonely. Why do they assume I am second rate, when I am, not! When I am not second rate? I mean has Shelley ever had a good review in his life? As for my life, I have never done one thing that is not decent, to anyone; or going on middling to decent! And look at them. Byron is an overweight alcoholic, Shelley is an anorexic, neurotic mess! The planet is bestrewn with their abandoned children, lovers of both sexes and wives! Shelley has tuberculosis, Byron has syphilis and these are the men whom the intelligent among us worship as angels of freedom. No. It was a privilege to be the friend of those two young, beautiful men, in the heyday of that summer. No. Yes. After all, I am paid five hundred pounds, by Byron's publisher, to write a diary of this summer. Dreadful time, no! Time of my life. My decent life. So!

The couples finish their kisses.

I entered the living-room of the Villa Diodati, that stormy night.

Ten Tiny Fingers, Nine Tiny Toes *by Sue Townsend*

England, the future. Society has now been divided into different classes with various rules and strictures. Only the upper classes are allowed to breed and the lower classes, of which Section 5 is the lowest, are treated like peasants, live in poverty and are forbidden the right to read, write or even have children.

Pete is a Section 5 living in Derbyshire. His wife, Dot, has fallen pregnant illegally and has been taken into hospital to give birth. The baby will be put down at birth. Pete is unemployed. In this speech Pete is waiting for news of Dot but is forbidden to visit her in hospital. In his loneliness he talks aloud to Dot . . .

_____

Pete I done like you said, I've been a good boy, careful with the wood, still got some and you been gone a long time. When you coming home Dot? (*Pause.*) A bloke on the fifteenth floor told me there's a job goin'. I don't now where but sounds all right eh? A chance anyway. He's goin' to try and find out – details – that sort of thing. I don't know who this bloke is. But, he was nice, you'd have taken a shine like I did. He looked all right. I an't been to see you Dot 'cos I don't know where you are. I went up to the roof last night, the wind nearly 'ad me. I tried to see Buxton then I 'ad to stop lookin' 'cos my eyes froze up. I 'ope you'll come back soon, 'specially now there's the chance of this job. I don't know his name, but I gave 'im mine. Pete Bird I said, that's my name. I told 'im which room it was. He didn't write it down. Will he remember or 'as 'e already forgot?

Pete *gets up from the fire. He goes and stands in front of the picture on the wall. As he speaks he points to the youths in the picture.*

. . . Barry, 'e were a big 'un. 'E could carry a post on 'is own. Glen, 'e were a black boy, 'is mam used to wrap 'is sandwiches dead tidy like she'd bought 'em in a shop. Martin, 'e left. Tony, 'e were a blabber mouth, always yakkin', 'e told lies an' all. Then me, Pete Bird, I were a good worker, never lost a minute. Allus turned up even when it were snowin'. My work were more important to me than owt else. It weren't just work, it were helpin'.

Come back 'ome Dot. I ain't feeling right. Sommat's missin'. It's like when me mum died, I'm not that fussed about the baby if the truth's known, I only want it 'cos you want it. We've done without it, we've got by. Come 'ome Dot.

After Haggerty *by David Mercer*

Bernard is a successful English lecturer. He moves into a new house but finds his life becomes affected by the previous owner, Haggerty, and the problems he has left behind.

Bernard regularly visits his elderly father. He struggles to communicate genuinely but more often than not falls prey to frustration and anger.

Bernard Dad – who can resist you? Who can resist a man who writes: 'Your Uncle Charlie's had his other leg off. A finer man never wore a pair of boots'? (*Pause.*) Look, I'm only trying to say the statement has its comic side. (*Pause.*) I *know* there's nothing funny about losing both your legs. For God's sake! (*Pause.*) Look, I was in the bloody, blasted war, you know! (*Pause.*) What? (*Pause.*) I've told you before. I got that wound in the arse when I was climbing out of a burning tank! It's not, cowardice-wise, a question of which way I was pointing, dad. (*Pause.*) How could I be running away from the Germans when the sods had us encircled? Go on! Tell me! And tell me, whilst we're at it, why you have to bring it up about three times a year? (*Pause.*) You've given me more scars talking about it than the actual piece of bloody shrapnel! (*Pause.*) I *know* it's not the same as Uncle Charlie. So he gets one chopped off down the pit, and one sawn off years later in hospital. I mean, I suppose the surgeon knew what he was doing. I just – (*Long pause.*) All right. I'll accept that. We'll try to stay off 'controversial topics'. Jesus. (*Long pause.*) Dad, you don't believe in God either so why get worked up about me saying Jesus? (*Long pause.*) Yes, I expect I am a bit tanned. I've been in Cuba. I wrote and told you I was *going*. All I can say is your memory for anything to do with me has *gone*. It simply doesn't function. (*Long pause.*) Well, I was a bit frightened of sharks. Sea's boiling with sharks around there. *And* barracuda. (*Long pause.*) Three and a half pounds, was it? A perch? Down at Crawston Dam. (*Pause.*) Dad. Don't say things like: 'From the sublime to the ridiculous'! Please. There is *no* contest on between my sharks and your perch. None whatsoever. (*Long pause.*) What? You thought Cuba was part of America and it's been and gone and gone communist?

Bernard *stands, looking in front of him woodenly. Long pause.*

Dad. Your mind doesn't have ideas. It has enigmatically related confusions. (*Pause.*) Sorry. (*Pause.*) I was about to say there was a sense in which Cuba was part of the USA. But it bloody well isn't any more. (*Long pause.*) Why are you crying? (*Pause.*) All my life I thought you were something like a mute. (*Pause.*) She did all the talking. (*Pause.*) Now *you* do the talking. (*Pause.*) And when you revert. When you go mute. Which is to say: when I begin to think I recognize you again – dammit, you cry! (*Long pause.*) Padre o muerte! Venceremos!

Crazy Gary's Mobile Disco *by Gary Owen*

Matthew D. Melody is a failed cabaret singer. Although he means well Matthew is on medication and his behaviour can often be misinterpreted as 'odd'. He often finds himself coming into conflict with people, from his next-door neighbours to the woman at the job centre. Matthew has fallen in love with Candy, who delivers singing telegrams and lives with a drug dealer. Candy is clearly using Matthew as a means of obtaining drugs but he doesn't realise this and genuinely believes they are in love.

This speech takes place on a karaoke evening when Matthew has just told Candy that he's told his doctor he no longer needs pills as he is in love.

Matthew 'I couldn't have done it without you, darling,' I tell her – and then the tape rolls, and it's my tune they're playing. I grab the mike from the compère's hand and jump on stage.

Croons at breakneck speed:

'YanevercloseyureyessanymorewhenIkissyuhlips . . .'

I settle into the rhythm.

Clicks his fingers lounge-lizard style, trying to find the beat.

'and there's no tenderness like before in your fingertips . . .'

And I look into Candy's loving eyes.

Pulls up sharply.

Except . . . they don't – look that loving. They're almost cold. Almost . . . contemptuous.

She's standing there, just in front of the stage, staring at me with these terrible cold eyes, slowly shaking her head . . .

I keep on singing but it has to be the worst performance of my life, cause I'm not feeling the music, I'm not even thinking about the music, I'm just thinking, Candy, Candy, what have I done wrong? How can you look at me with . . . *hatred* in your eyes? How? How?

My heart breaks.

I feel it breaking, like the ice on a lake when some little fat kid tries to go skating. And as that cold stare burns into me, I feel my heart freezing over, like the little fat kid turning blue at the bottom of the lake, and I know I will never love again.

The song comes to an end. Candy turns and walks out of the pub.

I hang my head. My life . . . is over.

And the crowd erupts into applause. The compère puts his arm around me, and there are tears in his eyes, and the thick lenses of his glasses magnify the tears so they're the size of marbles, and in the marbles I can see little rays from the spotlights, splitting up into all the colours of the rainbow, like the rainbow the Dear Lord God sent to Noah after the Flood, to tell him that the bad times were over and everything would be good from now on.

'Matthew,' says the compère. 'You were tremendous in the first heat, yeah, but that was spectacular. I don't think I've heard such an emotional reading of that song – in my life.'

And I begin to understand.

The compère's still going on.

'I don't think we need to,' he says. 'No. I don't think I can *bear* to hear any more. Nothing I could hear tonight could match that performance. That's it. That's it, everyone – the competition is over. Mathew D. Melody – you are the first ever Boar's Head Karaoke King!'

He sees the light.

She pretended! Candy pretended! She *pretended* she didn't love me any more – and scared me into giving the performance of my life.

She put herself through that . . . *torture*. For me.

'thank you,' I say to the compère. 'Thank you very much indeed. But now, if you'll excuse me, I've got to go. First, I've got to go and put a dangerous bottle safely away in a bin. And then I've got to go and find my true love.

Insignificance *by Terry Johnson*

Insignificance shows modern man's attempts to come to terms with his own mortality in the face of the nuclear threat. Four legends of Fifties America meet in a hotel room one night. The Ballplayer, loosely based on Joe DiMaggio, suspects his wife (Marilyn Monroe) of being unfaithful to him. In this speech he is talking to the Professor (Einstein) whilst waiting for his wife to come out of the bathroom.

———————————

Ballplayer Some punk kid thinks he's a bigshot, they put him on a bubble gum card.

He throws it away.

You know how many bubble gum series I been in? Thirteen. Thirteen series. I been in Chigley's Sporting Greats. I been in Pinky's World Series Stars 1936, 1937, 1939, 1942, 1944, 1945, 1949 and 1951. I been in Tip Top Boy's Best Baseball Tips showing how best to pitch, swing, deadstop and slide, and I have been Hubbly Bubbly's Baseball Bites best all-rounder nine years running. So no, hey! Hold on. That's 13 series but . . . 21 separate editions all told. And how many kids you know collect? Card for card it must run into millions. I must be stuck in albums from here to the Pacific. World wide. They gave gum to little Chink kids, don't they? You liberate them one day, next day they're making swops. I saw on TV they don't take beads and stuff up the Amazon no more; they take instant coffee and bubble gum. I could go into a little village in Africa that's hardly seen a white man and they'd say 'Hi Big Hitter, sit down and have some coffee.' This fame thing's enough to give you the heebies, I can tell you. Chigleys, Pinkys, Hubblys and Tip Top. That's some bubble gum.

The Memory of Water *by Shelagh Stephenson*

Northumberland, mid-winter. The three daughters of an elderly widow have gathered for her funeral. Over the course of two days the various family tensions, alliances and affections are all exposed and explored.

Mike is the married lover of Mary, one of the sisters. She wants to have a baby to the consternation of Mike, who has clearly regarded this affair as a 'fling' rather than an actual committed relationship. In this speech he finally reveals his true feelings about fatherhood to Mary . . .

———————

Mike I don't want a child, Mary! I don't want a child. I can't want one just because you do. Love and paternity aren't indivisible in my mind. When I say I love you it means I like you, I want to be with you, I want to go to bed with you, it means all sorts of things but it doesn't necessarily mean three children and Sainsbury's every Saturday for the next thirty years— [. . .] I can't help what happened before I met you! You might not like what I'm telling you, but I can't lie to make you feel better. I never wanted kids in the first place. They happened and now I love them but I don't want any more. It's not because I'm cold or selfish – at least no more than anyone else is – it's that I feel sucked dry by what people need from me [. . .] You're where I come to be equal, I come to you because you're not asking to be healed. Some people aren't paternal. It's not a crime. I'm one of them. If you're a woman and you take care of your own fertility, nobody argues. Well, I've taken care of mine. I didn't have a vasectomy because Chrissie's ill, I had it for me.

Silence.

But obviously, you know, if you *are* pregnant, I'll stick by you.

Cries from the Mammal House *by Terry Johnson*

Cries from the Mammal House is an allegorical tale of a zoo facing bankruptcy. The only animal capable of restoring the zoo's fortunes is a creature as fantastic as the dodo.

Dave is a passionate conservationist. He balances a child-like delight in saving endangered species with a sardonic Welsh wit. Here he is talking to his local helper whom he believes has no knowledge of English.

————————————

Dave The Pink Pigeon is the perfect example of natural selection at its worst. The real problem with breeding them is that they don't bloody like one another. Thanks to you we've now got six potential breeding couples; thirty-six possible combinations and no two of them can bear to stand on the same bloody branch, let alone fornicate. And look at that. Call that a nest? Call that a nest, you miserable bloody thing? And there's not one of them learnt that the only kind of egg you lay from a perch twelve feet above the ground is a scrambled one! They're the stupidest bloody species I've ever come across. As for this one, look at him. He's a pedigree bloody pigeon him, look. Pink as you like, but he's only tried to mate once in three weeks; and that was with his water dish. Come on boyo, make an effort. It's the survival of your species we're talking about. They think I'm mad. Who does he think he is, they say. We don't want to fuck. We don't like it. My mum and dad were decent, they never fucked, so why should I? They think I'm mad. I think I'm mad. Sometimes I wish you spoke English.

Boys' Life *by Howard Korder*

Phil, Don and Jake are all in their twenties, living in the US. The three men are all searching for fulfilment in relationships but have very differing attitudes. Jack is married but is looking for an affair, Don goes through a series of one-night stands and Phil cannot get over the recent end of his serious relationship.

In this speech he describes how his girlfriend finished their love affair.

———————————

Phil I would have destroyed myself for this woman. Gladly. I would have eaten garbage. I would have sliced my *wrists* open. Under the right circumstances, I mean, if she said, 'Hey, Phil, why don't you just cut your wrists open,' well, come on, but if *seriously* . . . We clicked, we connected on so many things, right off the bat, we talked about God for *three hours* once, I don't know what good it did, but that *intensity* . . . and the first time we went to bed, I didn't even touch her. I didn't *want* to, understand what I'm saying? And you know, I played it very casually, because, all right, I've had some rough experiences, I'm the first to admit, but after a couple of weeks I could feel we were right there, so I laid it down, everything I wanted to tell her, and . . . and she says to me . . . she says . . . 'Nobody should ever need another person that badly.' Do you *believe* that? 'Nobody should ever . . .'! What is that? Is that something you saw on TV? I dump my *heart* on the table, you give me Joyce Dr Fucking Brothers? 'Need, need,' I'm saying I *love* you, is that wrong? Is that not allowed any more? (*Pause.* **Jack** *looks at him.*) And so what if I did need her! Is that so bad? All right, crucify me, I needed her? So *what*! I don't want to be by myself, I'm by myself I feel like I'm going out of my mind, I do. I sit there, I'm thinking forget it, I'm not gonna make it through the next *ten seconds*, I just can't *stand* it. But I do, somehow, I get through the ten seconds, but then I have to do it all over again, 'cause they just keep coming, all these . . . seconds, floating by, while I'm waiting for something to happen, I don't know what, a car wreck, a nuclear war or something, that sounds awful but at least there'd be this *instant* when I'd know I was alive. Just once. 'Cause I look in the mirror, and I can't believe I'm really there. I can't believe that's me. It's like my body, right, is the size of, what, the Statue of Liberty, and I'm inside it, I'm down in one of the legs, this gigantic hairy leg, I'm scraping around inside my own foot like some tiny foetus. And I don't know who I am, or where I'm going. And I wish I'd never been born. (*Pause.*) Not only that, my hear is falling out, and that really *sucks*. (*Pause.*)

The Art of Success *by Nick Dear*

The Art of Success is set in Hogarth's London where
corruption, dissolution and disease are rife. In this climate
Hogarth is struggling to ensure a copyright on his
engravings.

Walpole is the Prime Minister and controls the entire
government by taking most public offices himself or giving
them to members of his family. In this speech he is trying
to write a play, having just made love to the Queen.

———————————

An apartment in a palace. A large, ornate bed. A woman lies in it.
Walpole, *half-dressed, sits at a nearby table, writing. He screws up a sheet of paper and throws it away.*

Walpole It's not as easy as I thought. The costume changes are a bugger. I need the heroine half-naked for the climax, so I've got to find a reason to get her off-stage and then I've got to find another reason to get her on-stage again. Give me the House of Commons any day.

He looks to the woman.

I know it won't be a popular law. But hang me a booming economy seems to breed subversion more than an age of hardship. It is precisely the popularity of the playhouses that renders them such a threat. Oh, I long to bring in a sensible, modern system, in which it is simply made plain to these chaps that it's in their own interests to toe the Lord Chamberlain's line. . . . A hint here. . . . A whisper there. . . . Get the Artistic Director in for a cup of tea, wave a small cheque in his face. . . .Just nudge the idea in. Where did the thinking spring from, that art must necessarily equal trouble? I am pacific, it is my nature, I believe with all my heart that what we need for the growth of the nation is peace. I don't like trouble and nor do the people. We like a quiet life and a decent dinner and why can't these toe-rags accept it? – Ah! Good!

He writes fast.

Get your costume off, you difficult old bag.

Five Kinds of Silence *by Shelagh Stephenson*

Billy has grown up as a physically and mentally abused child. He carries this abuse into his adult life and abuses his wife and children, literally keeping them locked inside the family home.

In this speech Billy describes one of his early experiences of child abuse and how he turned his fear into anger and violence.

———————————

Billy I don't remember pain, I don't remember pleasure. I was born aged six with teeth and a black, black heart. I'm what, eight? She has a new man now, a soft milky thing, no match for my lost blind dad. He winds wool for her with his limp fish hands. A voice like gruel. Boneless he is. And yet. And yet – Dark . . . feet like blocks of ice, heart bumping against my throat. Voices burbling in the blackness, Is anybody there? Is anybody there? They got a drowned man once, he spoke with weeds tangled in his throat, I heard him. He opens his mouth and it's not his voice come out it's dead people. Not frightened, me, I'm just cold, that's what that banging noise is in my chest. Dry tongue. Stupid bastards don't know I'm here. Stupid bastards. There's someone coming through, he says, there's someone coming through, it's a man. Stupid bastards, I don't believe them, I wish someone would put the light on the skin's going tight on the top of my head I think I'm having a heart attack. MAM! Billy? Is that you? Let me stay, I want to stay, I won't make no noise. I told you, bloody bugger, I told you. She's pulling me, dragging me upstairs, I'm fighting back, bloody get off me, bloody get off. No don't shut me up in the dark, it's black in there, the black gets in my nose and mouth and eyes, I can't breathe. She says get in the cupboard, you'll have no light, you don't deserve it. Bloody bugger bastard, I shout, bloody damn bugger. Crack. She hits me. Crack. Keep your fury, Billy, she says, you'll need it out there, but never cry, or I'll send the devil to you. No, no, I won't cry, don't send him, I don't want to see him, don't shut the door, what if he comes, Mam, what if he comes? But she slams the door anyway. I won't cry, I shout, I bloody won't. Bastards . . . bloody damn blast shit bastards . . . don't send the devil to me, I don't want to see him . . . bloody bugger pig devil, I bloody am not I bloody am not I bloody am not frightened you buggers – you pig buggers.

Ghostdancing *by Deepak Verma*

Ghostdancing is a reworking of *Thérèse Raquin*, updated to
the present-day Punjab.

Nitin, a some-time portrait painter, has embarked on an
affair with Rani, the repressed wife of his old school friend,
Raj. Carried away with passion for one another the lovers
have murdered Raj but, unable to come to terms wit their
guilt and haunted by the ghost of their victim, their lives
together have descended into accusation, recrimination
and violence. Raj's mother, Leila, has had a stroke and is
incapable of movement or communication although she is
aware of their crime.

In this speech Nitin has just strangled to death a pet
monkey who he was convinced had been possessed by the
soul of Raj. Clutching desperately at normality he chats to a
hate-filled Leila whilst preparing to paint the monkey's
corpse.

————————————

Nintin Are you hungry, Mother?

He waits for a response which he knows he will never get.

Nitin No? Well, it's just as well – she is not here and I can't cook. Shall I tell you something, Mother? I followed her today. I was afraid that she would go to the police station. But you would be happy, wouldn't you – if that is what she did? I followed her. She was wearing a flowing sari and she had put on her face the kind of make-up that foreign women wear . . . and she knew that every man on the street was looking at her. That is what she wanted . . . And do you know where she went? D'Souza Marg – where I had my bachelor home, remember? And I saw her hold the arm of a young man – he had a small moustache and a golden watch. He took her on his arm and they went into a lodging house. I thought I saw her through the window, with the man's hand on her breasts . . . I'm happy actually – you might not believe me, but I am happy. At least she's occupying herself. So I shall start doing the same thing myself – getting on with my life . . .

Dog *by John Hegley*

John Hegley is a performance poet and comedian. This
monologue is taken from a longer piece in which he talks
about his childhood, growing up in Luton.

_____

I had started to take an interest in the Town's football side after England's World Cup victory in '66. Being despised at school, I quickly clicked into soccer as a source of engagement, and my mum supported my support with growing fervour. Together we would watch for away results on the telly and leap from the three-piece seating if 'The Town' were announced to be the victors in a meeting.

Later I would attend many of these games, and it was through this travel that I would get a taste for the north of England, Bradford in particular, where I would later take up a university place. Getting the fares together for this jaunting was daunting on my mother's budget, but she always managed it. She would see excursions advertised weeks in advance and would ask me such questions as 'Do you want to go to Barrow, John?' An act of massive and total giving, the essence of parenthood. Home games I always attended and any match I went to would be followed by a detailed and impassioned debriefing on my return. She got to know the individual players' profiles intimately. The intimacy was always a knowing from afar. She never entered a football ground in her life, but many she entered in her imagining, and I believe that she and I were significantly responsible for Luton winning the Fourth Division Championship at the height of our involvement in 1968. The night they received the trophy we danced around the living room. Any boisterous activity in the home usually moved Hunter to barking and biting, but this time he was shut into grudging quietude as Mum and I festivalled like crazy; and she with the ribbons of *Sunday Times* fluttering from her now greying hair.

Herons *by Simon Stephens*

Billy is a fourteen year old living on an estate in East
London. He is a fundamentally decent child, trying to live a
normal life of school and pursuing his hobby of fishing. He
is bullied by a slightly older gang of boys. The leader of the
gang, Scott, believes that Billy's father grassed to the police
about a murder on the estate, sending Scott's older brother
to prison. As the time comes for the brother's release, Scott
and his gang step up their vendetta towards Billy with tragic
results.

In this speech Billy is trying to explain his sense of
disillusion and confusion to Scott's epileptic girlfriend,
Adele.

_____

Billy (*explaining*) I was leaving school one time last week. There was a lad waiting outside the school. An older lad. About eighteen. I watch him waiting at the bus stop. And he's waiting for a kid in Year Ten.

Billy *turns to confront her with his justification. She doesn't break eye contact with him.*

Billy As I'm coming out of the gates the kid in Year Ten is walking ahead of me and this lad gets him. This eighteen-year-old. Gets him. Gets him by his coat. And he pulls his head down and smacks it against a lamp-post. Four times. Back and down against the metal bit on the lamp-post. [. . .] I've seen teachers talk to kids as though they are worthless scabby shit. Bully them. Humiliate them. Never think about stopping and asking if they need help but instead, they just, instead they just say stupid cruel things. And the reason they do it is because so many of the kids, not all of them, but so fucking many are so fucking stupid and dick around and act like tossers. They think it's funny. It's not. It's shitty. And it ruins things. [. . .] I come down here, Adele Kent, and there is litter, pissy fucked litter everywhere. And it's kids that have left it. [. . .] Even here. Even the surface of the water. The place looks like it's fucking ripped up. People don't care. Do they? Even about trees and that? People just, why do they, just fucking, the way people treat trees around here is despicable!

Star Quality *by Christopher Luscombe, adapted from the play and short story by Noël Coward*

The 1950s. Ray, a director who had made a name for himself directing kitchen sink dramas, is hired to direct a play starring the hugely experienced, megalomaniac and self-involved actress, Lorraine Barrie. Throughout the rehearsal period Lorraine has behaved irresponsibly, arriving late for rehearsals, upsetting other members of the cast and generally behaving like a 'star'.

In this scene Lorraine has just confronted Ray after discovering that he intends to fire her old friend Marion. Lorraine has staged a weepy scene in front of the author and Ray, accusing him of not thinking about her needs as a performer and swearing undying loyalty to the play. Ray, not taken in for a moment, finally snaps and tells Lorraine the naked truth – something she hasn't heard for many years . . .

———————————

Ray (*mowing her down*) You sent for me because you wanted a nice satisfying scene, ending up with all of us in tears and me comforting you and telling you that you are the most glorious, God-given genius the theatre has ever known. Then we should have billed and cooed our way through the rest of the rehearsal – which, incidentally, you need just as much as the rest of the cast (**Lorraine** *lets out an involuntary moan.*) – and once firmly established on a nauseating kiss-and-be-friends basis, you would immediately have set to work again, insidiously and unscrupulously, to win back the point that you lost at the outset, namely that Marion should continue playing Stella, a part for which she is too old and entirely unsuited. It isn't even that she's bad. I can forgive a bad actress, and occasionally coax her into being a good one. But no. That poor, overpaid repertory hack is worse than bad; she's thoroughly and appallingly competent. There's no cheap technical trick that she doesn't know and use with sickening precision. No prayers, no exhortations, no carefully phrased explanations will budge her inner conviction that she knows how to do it, and what is so macabre is that she's right. She does know how to do it. But she knows how to do it *wrong* – she has always known how to do it wrong! In this particular part she is sweet, tolerant, understanding and lethal. She's a bloody murderess – she kills the character and the play stone dead with the first line she utters. And yet, Lorraine, you love her. Of course you love her! Any star would love Marion Blake: she's a megalomaniac's dream. She's a monumental bum-crawler, her clothes are catastrophic and she makes tea at matinées. But that isn't enough for me! All is ask is a decent, hard-working actress who can take direction and give proper value to the play – yes? The play you claim to love? – and the woods are full of them. One glance through *Spotlight* and I could find a dozen who would play the part perfectly. Yet here I am, landed with this superannuated, clacking soubrette because she offers you no challenge and no competition. You've wanted her in the cast from the first for one reason and one reason only, because she's a good foil to you and is shred enough to allow herself to be your offstage toady and bottle washer!

3 1221 07024 7544